How to Hold a Cockroach

A book for those who are free
and don't know it

Matthew Maxwell
Illustrations by Allie Daigle

Hearthstone

Published by Hearthstone®
www.thisishearthstone.com

Printed in the United States of America
ISBN 978-1-7333533-3-5

Cover design: Enrica Barberis
Illustration: Allie Daigle
Design/Art Direction: Enrica Barberis

To This, just as it is.

Thank you for reading *How to Hold a Cockroach,*
an offering from my heart to yours. I hope that the
boy's journey brings light, peace, and understanding
to your own. In appreciation, I have created an
audio companion to the book, and I share it with
you as a free gift. You will find details and a link
to it in the afterword. Enjoy!

With love,
Matthew Maxwell

Contents

Part One:

A Boy and His Stories

Chapter One
The Boy and A Cockroach

Once there was a boy who lived in his home alone. He sat at his table and ate dinner, generally feeling okay about things. As he sat contentedly chewing, he saw a cockroach crawl onto the table in front of him. It was big, brown, and disgusting. It frightened the boy. He screamed and shouted and wanted the cockroach to go away and never come back.

"Go away, cockroach!" he yelled. "Leave me alone!" But the cockroach just stood there, staring back. The boy hated cockroaches. He hated how they made him feel, anxious and grossed out.

The cockroach repulsed him so much that he couldn't eat. He felt this way whenever cockroaches invaded his space like this. *It makes me sick!* he thought. He wanted to smash

or get rid of it, but the bug was too nasty to get close to. It felt impossible.

The boy wondered what made him hate cockroaches so much. He had heard of people in a far-off land that eat cockroaches as snacks. They hold them in their hands with delight, like the boy might hold a strawberry. The thought made him squirm — he couldn't imagine holding a cockroach like that!

He remembered a time when he was very young. His mother saw a cockroach and shrieked. "Go away, cockroach!" she yelled. "Leave me alone!" It scared him to hear his mother scream like that. In that moment, he began to believe that cockroaches were gross, dangerous, and scary. Ever since then, he had noticed more and more evidence that it was true. How they would crawl up the wall when he least expected or sit waiting in the bathroom at night, with their scaly bodies and creepy antennae. And everyone else appeared to agree!

As time went on, the story seemed so true that he couldn't tell it was made up. It just became a fact: cockroaches are gross, dangerous, and scary. And here he was, this night at the table, experiencing the impact of what cockroaches had become to him. He was disgusted and upset.

He considered all this as he sat there, staring at the cockroach. His heart pounded in his chest.

Then a little miracle happened. The boy started to realize that he had been scared of the cockroach not for what it was, but for what he had believed it was. He questioned, for the first time in a very long time, how much he actually knew about cockroaches. *What are you, really?* he wondered. He looked at the cockroach with curiosity, the way he would have looked at it when he was a tiny boy, before his mother screamed. He began to feel compassion.

He thought, *Maybe cockroaches aren't all that different from me.*

Chapter Two
The Boy and Himself

That night, the boy stood in front of the mirror, brushing his teeth and looking at himself. He looked like a grown-up. He was big, brown-haired, and awkward. He frightened himself. In his mind, he screamed and shouted and wanted the person in the mirror to go away and never come back.

"Go away, boy!" he yelled. "Leave me alone!" But the face in the mirror just stood there, staring back. The boy hated looking in the mirror. He hated how it made him feel, disappointed and afraid.

He was so distressed by himself that he couldn't relax. He felt this way whenever thoughts of himself appeared. *I'm so messed up,* he thought. He wanted to fix himself, but he didn't know where to begin. It felt impossible.

The boy wondered what made him so frustrated with himself. He had heard of people who love themselves. They hold themselves in their hearts

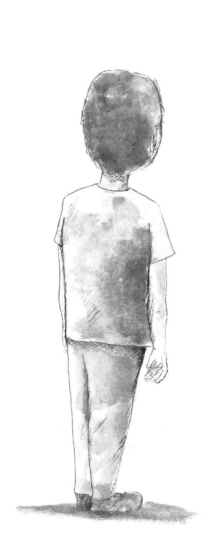
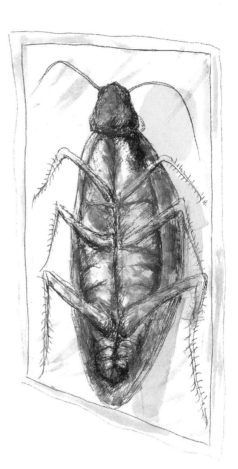

with care, like the boy might hold a spring blossom. That made him shiver — he couldn't imagine holding himself like that!

He remembered a time when he was very young. His mother saw him and shrieked. "Go away, boy!" she yelled. "Leave me alone!" It scared him to hear his mother scream like that. In that moment, he began to believe that he was bad, unwanted, and disliked. Ever since then, he had noticed more and more evidence that it was true. How he said mean things or acted stupidly; how people left when he arrived and looked at him when they whispered. Everyone appeared to agree!

As time went on, the story seemed so true that he couldn't tell it was made up. It just became a fact: the boy was bad, unwanted, and disliked. And here he was, this night at the mirror, experiencing the impact of what he had become to himself. He was miserable and ashamed.

He considered all this as he stood there, staring at himself. His face crinkled in distaste.

Then a little miracle happened. The boy remembered the cockroach, how he didn't know what it was. He started to realize that he had detested himself not for what he was, but for what he had believed himself to be and what he had believed others thought him to be. He questioned, for the first time in a very long time, how much he actually knew about himself. *What are you, really?* he wondered. He looked at the face in the mirror with curiosity, the way he would have looked at it when he was a tiny boy, before his mother screamed. He began to feel compassion.

Maybe I don't know who I am, he thought. *Maybe no one else does, either.*

Chapter Three
The Boy and Love

The boy went to his bedroom. He pulled a photograph from a dresser drawer, the picture of someone he had loved. He looked at the beautiful face. He used to feel such joy when he saw her, but now her picture filled him with anger and regret. In his mind, he screamed and shouted and wanted the memory of her to go away and never come back.

"Go away, love!" he yelled. "Leave me alone!" But the girl in the picture just stood there, staring back. The boy hated the picture. He hated how it made him feel, hopeless and hurt.

The memory of the girl upset him so much that he couldn't love. He felt this way whenever her memory invaded his mind like this. *It's too much!* he thought. He wanted to forget her and move on, but his heart wouldn't let go. It felt impossible.

The boy wondered what made him hate seeing her picture so much. He had heard of people who forgive the ones who leave them. They hold them

in their hearts with tenderness, like the boy might hold a precious heirloom. That made him clench — he couldn't imagine holding her like that.

He remembered the time when he last saw the girl. He said he loved her, and he asked her to return. But she turned him away. "Go away, boy!" she yelled. "Leave me alone!" It stunned him to hear someone he loved speak those words. In that moment, he began to believe that love was painful, dangerous, and scary. Ever since then, he had noticed more and more evidence that it was true. How love would break his heart when he least expected or never come to him at all; how the sweetest memories turned sour when loved ones left. And everyone else appeared to agree!

As time went on, the story seemed so true that he couldn't tell it was made up. It just became a fact: love was painful, dangerous, and scary. And here he was, this night in the bedroom, experiencing the impact of what love had become to him. He felt sad and alone.

He considered all this as he sat there, staring at the picture. His head dropped, and his face crumpled. A sob escaped his body, but he fought the tears back.

Then a little miracle happened. The boy remembered the cockroach, how he didn't know what it was. He started to realize that he had been hurt not by love nor by the girl, but by what he had believed about them and had made them mean. He questioned, for the first time in a very long time, how much he actually knew about the girl in the picture and how much he knew about love. *What are you, really?* he wondered. He explored love with curiosity, the way he would have looked at it when he was a tiny boy, before his heart first broke. He began to feel release.

Maybe it is okay that I loved her, he thought. *Maybe it is okay that I still love her.*

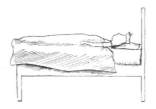

Chapter Four
The Boy and The Past

The boy yawned as he turned off the lights and laid himself down to sleep. It was now late. He thought of the day that had passed and its ups and downs. His thoughts turned to the past, all that had happened before now. It was heavy, dark, and disappointing. It saddened the boy. He clenched and resisted and wanted his memories to go away and never come back.

"Go away, past!" he pleaded. "Leave me alone!" But the past just stood there, staring back. The boy hated the past. He hated how it made him feel, frustrated and full of despair.

The past upset him so much that he couldn't sleep. He felt this way whenever it marched through his thoughts like this. *I've messed everything up!* he thought. He wanted to change how it all went, but there was no way to go back. It felt impossible.

The boy wondered what made him hate the past so much. He had heard of people with awful challenges who are at peace with how life has gone. They hold the past in their minds with gratitude, as the boy might hold a bowl of warm soup. That made him suspicious — he couldn't imagine relishing the past like that.

He remembered a time when he was very young. He tried to stand up to his mother, but that enraged his father, who shoved him to the ground. "Go away, boy!" his father yelled. "Leave her alone!" It had scared him to feel his father push like that. In that moment, he began to believe that what had happened was unfair and tragic, filled with mistakes and regret. Ever since then, he had noticed more and more evidence that it was true. How he tried and failed at his attempts; how others ended up angry and disappointed with him; how often things just didn't work out. And everyone else appeared to agree!

As time went on, the story seemed so true that he couldn't tell it was made up. It just became a fact: the past was unfair and tragic, a heap of mistakes and regret. And here he was, this night in the bedroom, experiencing the impact of what the past had become to him. He was hopeless and sad.

He considered all this as he lay there, staring at the past. His chest heaved, and his throat tensed.

Then a little miracle happened. The boy remembered the cockroach. He started to realize that he had been depressed not by the past itself, but by his interpretations about it. He questioned, for the first time in a very long time, how much he actually knew about the past. *What are you, really?* he wondered. He looked at what had happened with curiosity, the way he would have looked at it when he was a tiny boy, before his father first shoved him. He began to feel forgiveness.

Maybe there isn't a way things should have been,
he thought. *There is just the way things are.*

Chapter Five
The Boy and The Future

The boy opened his eyes and discovered that it was the next morning. He had fallen asleep, wondering about the past. He yawned and stretched his body in the shape of a star. As he lay there staring at the ceiling, his thoughts turned to the day ahead. It seemed long, dreadful, and grim. It agitated the boy. His mind continued anticipating, forecasting the future, the difficulties of the days and years to come. He screamed and shouted and wanted the future to go away and never come back.

"Go away, future!" he yelled. "Leave me alone!" But the future just stood there, staring back. The boy hated the future. He hated how it made him feel, worried and alone.

He dreaded the day ahead so much that he couldn't rise from his bed. He felt this way whenever the future invaded his mind like this.

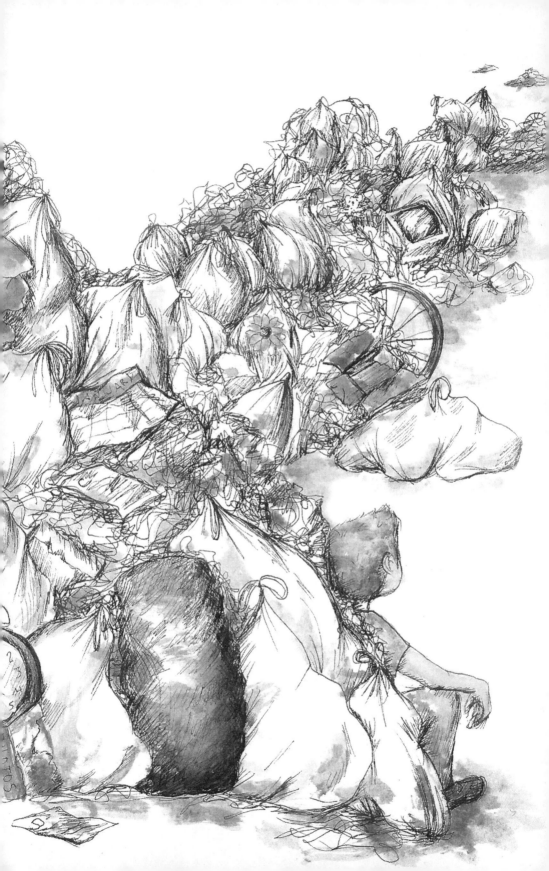

How will I get through this? he thought. He wanted to enjoy the future, but it seemed so grim. It felt impossible.

The boy wondered what made him dread the future so much. He had heard of people who look forward to life. They hold what's coming with anticipation, like he would hold an unopened present. That made him cringe — he couldn't imagine holding the future like that.

He remembered a time when he was very young. He woke up excited for a party planned for that evening. But he fell asleep early and missed the party completely. "Go away, boy!" the party-goers seemed to yell. "Leave us alone!" It disappointed him so much to miss the party like that. He began to believe that the future is disappointing and doesn't turn out like we hope. Ever since then, he had noticed more and more evidence that it was true. How things didn't go as planned and expectations failed; how it was best not to hope at all. And everyone else appeared to agree!

As time went on, the story seemed so true that he couldn't tell it was made up. It just became a fact:

the future is disappointing and does not turn out like we hope. And here he was, lying in his room at dawn, experiencing the impact of what the future had become to him. He was anxious and depressed, wanting a better future but afraid that his choices would just make things worse.

He considered all this as he lay there, dreading the day to come. He sighed heavily.

Then a little miracle happened. The boy remembered the cockroach. He started to realize that he had been scared of the future not for what it was, but for what he had believed it would be — more of the mistakes and disappointments of the past. He questioned, for the first time in a very long time, how much he actually knew about the future. *What else could you be?* he wondered. He looked at the future with curiosity, the way he would have looked at it when he was a tiny boy, before a dream was first dashed. He began to feel hope.

Maybe today will be like days past, he thought. *Or maybe it will be different.*

Chapter Six
The Boy and Doing

The boy got up to eat breakfast. He sat at his
table alone, generally feeling okay about things.
As he sat contentedly munching, he saw his
to-do list crawl onto the table in front of him —
people to speak with, chores to perform, errands
to run, assignments to complete, all he had
said he would do and hadn't. It overwhelmed
the boy. He screamed and shouted and wanted
the tasks to go away and never come back.

"What is all this?!" he yelled. "I can't take this
anymore!" But the list just stood there, staring
back. The boy hated always having to do things.
He hated how it made him feel: buried, trapped,
and resentful.

The things to do overwhelmed him so much
that he wanted to run away and never come
back. He felt this way whenever he thought
of all there was to do. *I hate this!* he thought.

He had to get all the things done, but there was too much, he didn't know how, and he didn't want to. It felt impossible.

The boy wondered what made him dread all these tasks so much. He had heard of people who enjoy what they do. They do their work with fun and ease, like the boy would slide down a slide. That made him jealous — he couldn't imagine enjoying his work like that!

He remembered a time when he was very young. He worked hard on a homework assignment and felt proud bringing it to school. "What is all this?!" his teacher admonished. "Do it again, and do it right next time!" It surprised him to hear his teacher reprimand him like that. It made him feel embarrassed and sad. In that moment, he began to believe that tasks must be done and they must be done right. Ever since then, he had noticed more and more evidence that it was true. How so much was asked of him, how he was praised when he did it well and scolded when he did not. And everyone else appeared to agree!

As time went on, the story seemed so true that he couldn't tell it was made up. It just became a fact: tasks must be done and they must be

done well. And here he was, this morning at breakfast, experiencing the impact of what doing had become to him: constantly plotting and planning, remembering all there was to do, figuring out how to do it and not mess it up.

He considered all this as he sat there, staring at the list of things to do. His lungs inhaled shallow breaths.

Then a little miracle happened. The boy remembered the cockroach. He started to realize that he felt afraid of doing and not-doing not for what they were, but for what he had believed about them. He questioned, for the first time in a very long time, what actually had to be done. *What is doing anyway?* he wondered. He looked at doing with curiosity, the way he would have looked at it when he was a tiny boy, before his homework was first criticized. He began to feel compassion.

Maybe some things have to be done and maybe they don't, he thought. *And who decides if they're done right?*

Chapter Seven
The Boy and Others

Later that morning, the boy drove in his car, generally feeling okay about things. As he sat contentedly driving, he saw traffic up ahead. His car slowed down to a halt, trapped by the long line of vehicles ahead. The traffic was vexing and stupid. It infuriated the boy. He screamed and shouted and wanted the people and their cars to go away and never come back.

"Come on, people!" he yelled. "Get out of my way!" But the traffic just stood there, staring back. The boy hated traffic, and he hated the people causing it. He hated how they made him feel, agitated and anxious.

He was so repulsed by the people in their cars that he couldn't stand to be around them. He felt this way whenever others got in his way like this. *Let me through, people!* he thought. He wanted to get where he was going, but the traffic was too dense to navigate. It felt impossible.

The boy wondered what made him hate everyone so much. He had heard of people who cherish others, even when they get in the way. He had seen people who sit in traffic with cheerfulness, like the boy would sit with a piña colada. That made him scoff — he couldn't imagine sitting in traffic like that!

He remembered a time when he was very young. He was waiting in line, and an older boy pushed him aside. "Come on, boy!" the bully threatened. "Get out of my way!" It had frightened him to be pushed aside like that. In that moment, he began to believe that people are mean and out to get him. Ever since then, he had noticed more and more evidence that it was true. How traffic always showed up at the worst times; how people acted rudely and said mean things; how they took things from him and kept him from what he wanted. And everyone else appeared to agree!

As time went on, the story seemed so true that he couldn't tell it was made up. It just became a fact: people are mean and out to get him.

And here he was, this day in the traffic,
experiencing the impact of what people had
become to him. He was angry and alone.

He considered all this as he sat there, staring
at the cars ahead. He banged his head against
the steering wheel.

Then a little miracle happened. The boy
remembered the cockroach. He started to realize
that he had been mad at people not for what they
were, but for what he had believed them to be.
He questioned, for the first time in a very long
time, how much he actually knew about others.
What are we, really? he wondered. He looked at
the people around him with curiosity, the way
he would have looked at them when he was
a tiny boy, before he was first pushed aside.
He began to feel compassion for them.

Maybe I'm not just stuck in traffic, he thought.
I'm stuck in all of these stories, too.

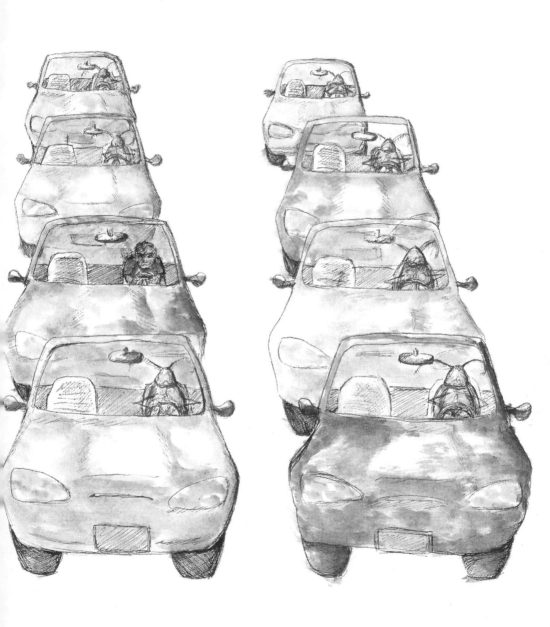

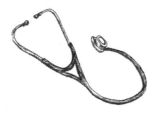

Chapter Eight
The Boy and Death

Eventually, the traffic passed, and the boy
arrived at his appointment. He waited for
a long time in a hospital room.

He tried not to be afraid, but he was.
The doctor appeared with a somber face.

The doctor shared the results of a recent
medical test. He said that the results were not
good and the boy may not survive for long.

The doctor left the room. The boy saw a cockroach crawling on the wall. It didn't matter to him though, because death had appeared. Death was dark and dense, the most horrible thing of all. It terrified the boy.

He froze and wanted death to go away and never come back. "Go away, death." he whispered. "Leave me alone!" But death just stood there, staring back. The boy hated death. He hated how it made him feel. He was in shock.

He was so aghast at the idea of his death that he could barely breathe. He felt this way whenever thoughts of death arose, but death had never seemed so close as it did now. *This just doesn't make sense, he thought.*

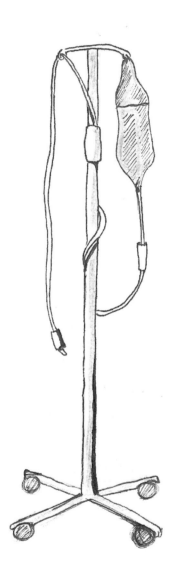

He wanted to treat his illness, but it might be
too painful. And what if it didn't work?
It felt impossible.

The boy wondered what made him hate death so
much. He had heard of people in a far-off land
that honor death. They greet it with peace and
patience, like the boy would greet an old friend.
That made him tremble — he couldn't imagine
greeting death like that!

He remembered a time when he was young. His
grandmother had become very sick. The boy
and his family gathered around her until, finally,
she took her last breath. The boy's grandfather
sobbed at her side. "Go away, death!" he cried.
"Leave her alone!" It had scared him to hear
his grandfather cry like that. In that moment,
he began to believe that death was terrifying
and awful, to be dreaded over everything else.
Ever since then, he had noticed more and more
evidence that it was true. How death came
suddenly or at the end of long illness, how

it visited young and old, how no matter when it came, it did not come when it should. And everyone else appeared to agree!

As time went on, the story seemed so true that he couldn't tell it was made up. It just became a fact: death was terrifying and dreadful. And here he was, this day in the doctor's office, experiencing the impact of what death had become to him. He was terrified. He considered all this as he sat there, staring at the medical report. His chest and lungs barely moved.

Then a little miracle happened. The boy remembered the cockroach. He started to realize that he had been scared of death not for what it was, but for what he had believed it to be. He questioned, for the first time in a very long time, how much he actually knew about death. *What are you, really?* he wondered. He looked at death with curiosity, the way he would have looked at it when he was a tiny boy, before his grandmother died. He began to feel grace.

Maybe my death is coming,
and maybe it will come soon,
he thought.

But it is not here now.

Chapter Nine
The Boy and Life

The boy went to the hospital cafeteria and sat
at a table alone. He ate lunch, generally feeling
horrible about things. He thought of death and
what it would be like to die, how it might be not
to live. As he sat slowly chewing, he became
mad at life for how it was. Life had been painful,
boring, and lonely. It infuriated the boy. He
seethed and cursed and wanted life to either be
worth living or to go away and never come back.

"Come on, life!" he ranted. "Give me a break!"
But life just stood there, staring back. The boy
hated life. He hated how it made him feel. He
felt furious and outraged.

He was so angry at life that death almost
seemed preferable. He felt this way whenever
life seemed this dark. *What is the point of all this?!*
he thought. He wanted to enjoy living, but life so
often felt miserable. He didn't know how to stop
suffering. It felt impossible.

The boy wondered what made him hate life so much. He had heard of people who love their life. They live with joy and ease, like the boy might float on a tube down a mountain stream. That made him angry — he couldn't imagine experiencing life like that!

He sensed a time when he was very young, so young that he could barely remember. Someone became very angry at him, when he was just a baby. He could not remember who

it was or what they said, just a flash of angry rage, directed at him. It terrified him to be the subject of such hostility, and the terror had been there ever since. In that moment, he began to believe that life hated him, that he must protect himself from it, that it was an ordeal to endure. Ever since then, he had noticed more and more evidence that it was true. How cockroaches showed up and ruined good meals, how traffic appeared at the worst times, how parties went

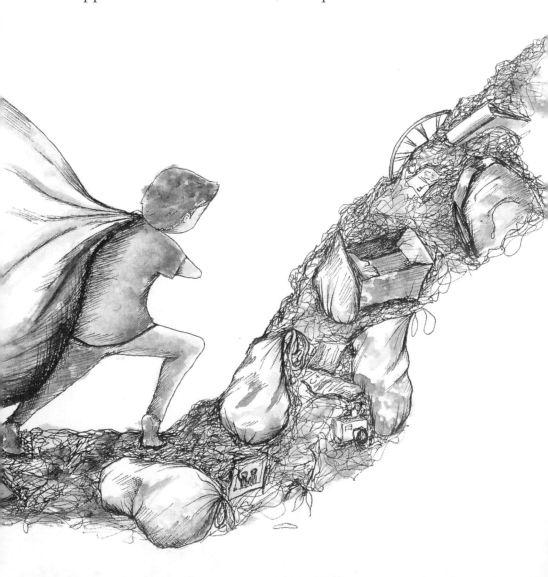

on without him and love crushed his heart. How life was so often full of pain and even the good moments, when they came, were fleeting and far between. *That's just how life is,* he so frequently thought, frustrated and resigned. And everyone else appeared to agree!

As time went on, the story seemed so true that he couldn't tell it was made up. It just became a fact: life was against him, a threat to protect from, a burden to endure. And here he was,

this day in the cafeteria, experiencing the impact of what life had become to him. He was isolated, afraid, and exhausted.

He considered all this as he sat there, staring at life. His fists clenched, and his jaw tightened.

Then a little miracle happened. The boy remembered the cockroach. He started to realize that he had been angry at life not for what it was, but for what he had believed it to be. He questioned, for the first time he could ever remember, how much he actually knew about life. *What is this, really?* he wondered. He looked at living with curiosity, the way he looked at things when he was just a baby, before that first memory of terror. He began to feel compassion.

Maybe life means whatever we think it does, he thought. *Or maybe it means nothing at all.*

Chapter Ten
The Boy and Emotion

The boy drove from the hospital to a trail in the woods. He had a job, but work didn't make sense on a day like this. He sat on a bench and stared at the trees and the grass, considering death and considering his life. He looked back at all that had happened and what it all meant. As he sat there brooding, he felt emotions take hold of his body. They were deep and over-powering. They frightened the boy. He clenched and resisted and wanted the emotions to go away and never come back.

"Go away, feelings!" he insisted. "Don't come back until you're done!" But the emotions became even stronger, filling his chest and gut. The boy hated emotions. He hated how they made him feel. He felt nauseous and out-of-control.

The emotions scared him so much that he couldn't just be. He felt this way whenever

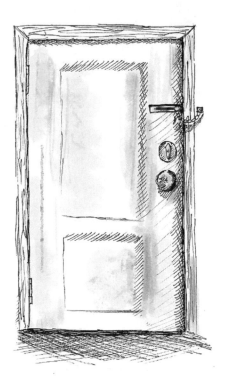

strong emotions tried to take him over like
this. *I just can't!* he thought. He wanted to
feel better, to distract himself from the pain,
but the emotions were too intense to ignore.
It felt impossible.

The boy wondered what made him hate
emotion so much. He had known people
who easily cry and express their anger.
They allow their emotions to flow through
them, like the boy would stand in a stormy
rain. That made him tense— he couldn't
imagine allowing his feelings like that!

He remembered a time when he was very young. Something scared him, and he began to cry. "Go away, crybaby!" his older sister commanded, sending him to his room. "Don't come back until you're done!" It humiliated him to be yelled at and banished like that. In that moment, he began to believe that emotions were bad and embarrassing, that there was something wrong with him for having them. Ever since then, he had noticed more and more evidence that it was true. How emotions made him feel terrible, how others laughed at those who cried, how people said or did awful things when anger aroused them. And everyone else appeared to agree!

As time went on, the story seemed so true that he couldn't tell it was made up. It just became a fact: emotions are bad and embarrassing, and there was something wrong with him for having them. And here he was, this day at the bench, experiencing the impact of what emotions had become to him, tense and tired from stuffing down the anger and sadness.

He considered all this as he sat there, holding in the emotions. His jaw began to quiver.

Then a miracle happened. He could hold the feelings down no longer. The fear of death, the pain of heartbreak, the overwhelm of doing, the challenge of life — it finally became too much to ignore. He buried his face in his hands and began to weep. He sobbed the tears of the boy

whose mom first told him to leave her alone, of
the man whose heart had been broken by love.
He cried for the boy who missed the party and
the man whose doctor told him that death was
near. He cried until the tears stopped, no longer
held back by the story of what they meant.

He took a deep breath. It was a deeper breath
than he had taken in a very long time.

Then he began to shake with rage. The anger
of the boy who hated looking at himself in the
mirror, whose father pushed him to the ground.
He felt rage for the boy who had been cast aside
and lived his life alone. Anger buried deep in
his body, that he had never let himself feel. His
body trembled and shook. He ran deeper into
the woods. He grabbed a tree branch from

the ground and slammed it into the dirt, over and over, roaring and yelling "No! No! NO!" until the branch finally broke and there was nothing left to yell.

The boy stood there in surprise, breathing heavily, his body finally released from the tension it had stored for so long. He began to cry again, now more gently. He started to realize that he had been scared of emotions not for what they were, but for what he had believed they meant. He questioned, for the first time in a very long time, how much he actually knew about feelings. *What are you, really?* he wondered. He sensed the energy in his body with curiosity, the way he would have felt it when he was a tiny boy, before he was first criticized for crying. He began to feel spacious.

Maybe feelings are meant to be felt, he thought. *And there's nothing wrong with us for feeling them.*

Chapter Eleven
The Boy and Knowing

The boy walked back to the bench on the trail. He sat again, staring at the trees and the grass, free from the hold of his emotions. He thought of what might come. He thought of all the things he thought he knew but maybe did not. His mind filled with doubt, as he contemplated what he didn't know: what life was, how close death was, whether any of it had a purpose. Not-knowing was terrifying. It frightened the boy. He fumed and fussed and wanted not-knowing to go away and never come back.

"C'mon, boy!" he said. "Don't be stupid." But not-knowing just stood there, staring back. The boy hated not knowing. He hated how it made him feel, terrified and adrift.

He was so nauseated by not-knowing that he wanted to disappear. He felt this way whenever uncertainty invaded his space like this. *I should know better!* he thought. He wanted to figure it all out, but everything seemed so unsettled. It felt impossible.

The boy wondered what made him hate not-knowing so much. He had heard of people who don't mind not-knowing. They hold the unknown with calm, like the boy would wade in the ocean. The thought made him sneer — he couldn't imagine being in the unknown like that!

He remembered a time when he was very young. He answered a question and got it wrong. The other children laughed and made fun of him. "C'mon, boy!" they yelled. "Don't be stupid!" It embarrassed him so much to hear them laugh like that. In that moment, he began to believe that he must always know and be right. Ever since then, he had noticed more and more evidence that it was true. How others complimented him when he knew things and made fun when he didn't. How much people liked him when they agreed with him and rejected him when they didn't. How being right helped him seem important and stay in control. And everyone else appeared to agree!

As time went on, the story seemed so true that he couldn't tell it was made up. It just

became a fact: he must always know and
be right, and terrible things would happen
if he didn't. And here he was, this day
on the bench, experiencing the impact of
what needing-to-know had become to him:
desperately seeking solutions to questions
with no answers, panicked and distraught.

He considered all this as he sat there, staring
at the trees and listening to the sound
of his heart.

Then a little miracle happened. The boy
remembered the cockroach. He started to
realize that he had been scared of not-knowing
not for what it was, but for what he believed
it meant. He questioned, for the first time in
a long time, how much he really knew about
knowing, and how much his knowing knew
about anything. *What is knowing, anyway?* he
wondered. He looked at not-knowing with
curiosity, the way he would have looked at it
when he was a tiny boy, before the children
first laughed at him. He began to feel peace.

*Maybe it is good at least to know that I do not
know,* he thought. *Or do I even know that?*

Chapter Twelve
The Boy and Everything

The boy walked to a patch of grass, a clearing amid the trees. He sat down, contemplating everything that had happened since seeing the cockroach at dinner the night before. He reflected on the things he had believed but maybe weren't so: that cockroaches are gross; that he was bad and unlovable; that the past is tragic, the future is dreadful, and love is pain; that things must be done and emotions suppressed; that life and death are enemies and others are, too.

He began to consider other stories he had believed, interpretations that had become the truth. That old people are dull and children are annoying and out-of-control. That work is boring and play is fun; that sickness means weakness and throwing up means you're gross. That men should be strong and women should be pretty. That money makes you happy;

not having it makes you a failure, but having too much makes you selfish and evil. That there are things people can do or can't and things they should do or shouldn't. That some choices are good and right and others are bad and wrong. That there was a way the world should be, but it was not that way. And the more he believed anything, the more evidence of it he noticed, until it all became true. *That's just how it is*, he had thought so many times. *And isn't that a shame.*

And here he was, this day in the woods, finally seeing the impact of what he had believed. Fear, despair, anger, regret, shame, and misery. Afraid to connect, love, and discover. Afraid to die and afraid to live. He was free but didn't know it: trapped by the walls of his interpretations and stories, the perpetual trance of his self-constructed reality.

Now, he wondered. He didn't know what cockroaches or people were. He didn't know what the past meant or the future would bring. *What are the past and future, after all,*

but ideas we carry around in our heads? As events
occurred, he had invented or agreed with
what they meant and walked through life as
if that meaning was true. That a thing is good
or bad, to be regretted or celebrated, cried over
or laughed at — all of it based on what he had
chosen or been taught to believe.

What are we? What is this? What is anything? he
wondered as he sat there, staring at the trees.

He considered how what he had believed —
all that seemed true about himself and
everything else — had caused him to suffer.
How his mind's need to be right about its
judgments had magnified the suffering. He
was so afraid to take chances, so unwilling
to risk, and so wary of love; held low by
the imaginary weight of failures past and
tragedies future, protecting and defending
against the terrifying mirages he feared the
most: that he was hated and disliked, not good
and not good enough; that he was too much or
too little, disappointing and stupid, shameful
and worthless.

And what his soul most desired —
connection, belonging, fulfillment —
a partner, a family, community — a life
of meaning, joy, and purpose — his
deepest desires were all out of reach,
impossible to experience from the
prison of his beliefs.

The boy's lungs heaved. He was tired of
the suffering. It wasn't worth it anymore.
Death was knocking, and he wanted to savor
however much of life remained. He wanted to
be happy more than he wanted to be right.

The boy laid down in the grass. He closed
his eyes, embraced by the part of himself that
knew love and compassion. "It's all okay,"
he heard himself say. "I love you. You're not
alone." He stepped through the fear and out
of his stories.

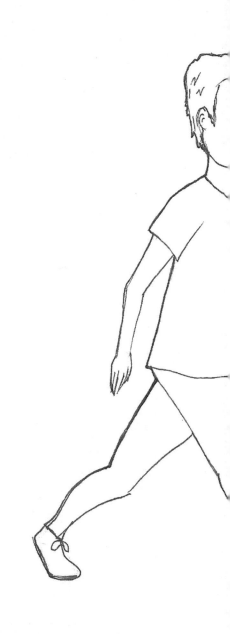

Part Two:

A New World

He lies here for a long time, with closed eyes.

Breathing in the dark.

Noticing how it feels to be.

Nothing is here.

Nothing to do. Nowhere to go. No one to be.

After a while, the boy opens his eyes.

Being

There are colors, lines, waves, movement.

Sounds in his ear, wind on his skin, sensations within.

He feels it all as if feeling it for the first time, like a baby waking up after a long nap. Without meaning or labels, without stories about what it is or isn't. There is just wonder and awareness.

He knows nothing and feels as if there is nothing to know. Nothing but the blissful awareness of curiosity for each moment and for the stunning miracle of existence. He smiles in joy. He wonders at the experience of being, at being aware of being. And being aware of the awareness!

The Choice

Little by little, his mind pieces together what
his senses perceive. Blowing colors become
green and brown and then turn into a tree.
Trilling delight becomes the song of birds.
Sprinkling rush becomes the nearby stream.

He is in the woods near his home, seeing
trees he has seen before as if he has never
before seen them. As if he has never seen any
tree. His heart stirs. He begins to cry with joy,
as he discovers something he has never quite
realized before: How beautiful it all is.

He looks to his side and sees a small, brown
creature in the grass. He remembers that he
once called this kind of creature a cockroach.
That he used to be frightened of it.

He doesn't know what the thing is. He
doesn't know what he is. He doesn't know
what anything is. He doesn't know what
knowing is.

But you can choose how to hold it! says the voice of compassion in his heart. *No matter what happens, whatever truth there may be, you can choose how to hold it.*

The boy thinks of his mother's scream, his dad's shove, and the doctor's report. He holds with compassion the one who experienced those things. He sees not a boy who messed up but a boy who cares. He tells him that he loves him no matter what, that he is sorry for his suffering. He tells the boy that he is light and joy, life's gift to itself. He tells him that people flow in and out of our lives, like cockroaches that come and go, and we can love them for whatever they are and forgive whatever they aren't. He tells him that life is a gift. And death makes it more precious!

You always have a choice, says the voice in his heart. To hold the past and future as you choose. To hold life as you choose. To hold yourself as you choose. *You always have a choice.*

"And the way I choose is love," says the man, as he embraces the boy within.

Saying that, the man begins to notice evidence of love. He remembers the boy who wrestled playfully with his father, danced freely to music, and sang along to his favorite songs. He remembers the parents who gently cared for him when ill; he remembers the meals and shelter life has always provided him. He thinks of hugs from friends and the guidance of mentors. He feels the relaxing comfort of a deep breath. He remembers the beauty of sunsets, the majesty of mountains, and the enchantment of looking into another's eyes. He sees the greens, browns, and blues all around him. He notices how it is to be him, to be here, to be love.

He sits up in the grass, taking in the world and the new possibilities arising in his soul.

Maybe everything is sacred, he thinks with a reverent breath. *Or maybe nothing is!*

He laughs in glee, reborn. The creator and witness of his world.

Epilogue
The Boy and A Cockroach

Some time later, the boy sits at his table and eats dinner, generally feeling okay about things. As he sits contentedly chewing, he sees a cockroach crawl onto the table in front of him. It is charming, cute, and fun. It delights the boy. He cheers and coos and wants the cockroach to stay and never leave.

"Greetings, beautiful cockroach!" he says. "You're welcome here!" The cockroach just stands there, staring back. The boy loves the cockroach. He loves how it makes him feel, joyful and at ease.

The cockroach delights him so much that he doesn't want it to leave. He feels this way whenever a guest warms his home like this. *It makes me happy!* he thinks. He watches to see what the cockroach will do next. Nothing feels impossible.

The boy wonders what makes him love cockroaches so much. He has heard of people in a far-off land who treat cockroaches as

emblems of deity. They hold them in their hands with reverence, the same way the boy now does. The thought makes him smile.

He remembers a time not too long ago. He saw a cockroach and chose how to hold it. "Greetings, beautiful cockroach!" he said. "You're welcome here!" It filled him with love to hear himself speak like that. In that moment, he began to believe that cockroaches were friends who are charming and kind. Ever since then, he has noticed more and more evidence that it is true. How they crawl up the wall when one least expects or sit waiting in the bathroom at night, with their sleek bodies and playful antennae. Hardly anyone appears to agree with him, but that is okay!

The story seems true, but he never forgets that it is made up. It is not a fact, just a possibility he likes to believe: cockroaches are charming, cute, and precious. And here he is, this night at the table, experiencing the impact of what cockroaches have become to him. He is happy and free.

He considers all this as he sits there, looking
at the cockroach. His lips widen in a smile.

The boy recognizes that he loves the cockroach
not just for what it is, but for the possibility
he has chosen to believe about it. The boy
reaches down and picks up the cockroach.
He holds it gently in his hands. It is sacred to
him. He questions, as he frequently does, how
much he actually knows about cockroaches.
What are you, really? he wonders. He looks at
it with curiosity, the way he looks at all of life
nowadays. He places the cockroach down,
and it scurries on its way. His heart is filled
with compassion.

He thinks, *Maybe cockroaches aren't all that
different from me.*

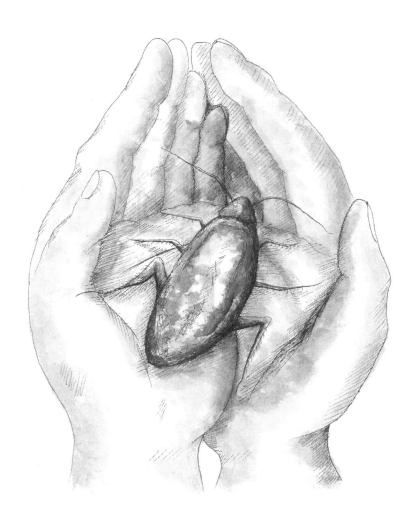

Afterword

**A note to my children,
whom I have not yet met**

This book is for you. What I want most for
you is to have a life of joy: connecting to
others with ease and depth, creating what
you yearn for, and experiencing fulfillment
and satisfaction, day-to-day and moment-
by-moment. I write with conviction that it
is possible to experience life this way.

This book is about creation and destruction.
It is about power and stagnancy. It is about
love and fear. It is about life being wonderful,
horrible, exactly as you would like, or nothing
like you would like.

This book was written to give you the option
of experiencing the life you dream of, to
shape yourself and the world according to
your heart's desire. It is about the power of
our beliefs, and the message is this: We can
choose what things are to us, what they mean,
and how to hold them. To do this, we may

need to "un-know" some of what our minds hold as true. I believe that if you'll consider this message and play with it from a place of openness, discovery, and love, you'll be free to experience your deepest desires.

Finally, in the spirit of this message, let me share who you are to me. You are angels, embodiments of the greatest light and love of the universe. You are goddesses, with the divine spark of creation. You are brilliance, play, wonder, delight, joy, and power. You are the future of humanity, and with your light and love, humanity and the earth will be well taken care of.

May your lives be filled with love, may you find joy in what you create and what comes to you, and may your paths be light. I love and accept you, exactly as you are, right now and always.

Your devoted father,
Matthew

A note to the reader

I imagined you — the unknown you — many times as I wrote this book, desiring that the boy and his journey would make a difference for you and your life. I have debated what else to share. On one hand, I desire to let the story impact you however it does and simply bless that. On the other, I wish for you to experience (or experience anew) a similar journey, and sometimes an invitation brings us where we otherwise might not go. So, I suggest some steps to explore, perhaps in a journal or to share out loud with a friend.

1) Select something that seems problematic to you — cockroaches, yourself, a current or past situation, anything.

2) What emotions arise about it? Allow them to be fully felt.

3) What has become true about this for you? What is the impact of believing this way?

4) Now, breathe deeply, and bring yourself here, to this moment. Invite yourself out of what you've "known," and examine the thing/person/situation/idea as if you had never experienced it before. See it through the eyes of an infant. What do you notice? What else might be true about the thing?

5) Choose how to hold it!

If you'd like to connect, visit HowtoHoldaCockroach.com. There you can learn more about my work as a coach and speaker, sign up to receive updates and inspiring messages, connect on social media, or send me a message directly. I'd love to hear about the "cockroaches" in your life and how you've chosen to hold them. You can also find out more about workshops, courses, and other opportunities for exploring the themes of this book, including the How to Hold a Cockroach Retreat!

Finally, I trust that this book will journey to the hands and hearts of those who need it most — we who are free and forget it. If you feel inspired to share a copy, please do.

With love and appreciation,
Matt Maxwell

P.S. With gratitude, I share a free gift: the audio version of this book! The captivating voice of Simon Vance and original music by producer Mason Maxwell make it a special experience. I think you'll love it. Download it for free at HowtoHoldaCockroach.com/CockroachAudioGift

Acknowledgments

My deepest gratitude to:

Mom and Dad. You are not responsible for the stories I believed as you did your magnificent best. Thank you for blessing me with the marvelous gift of life.

My sisters and brothers, my team for life. Megan, a heart-shaped rock. Mindy, a daring spark. Mark, a gentle shoulder to lean on. Mason, a dream maker (and a crucial assistant in creating this book).

Cheri Huber and Ashwini Narayanan, who guide the work of Living Compassion, and the monks of the Zen Monastery Peace Center. Thank you for inviting us to see ourselves through the eyes of love.

Stacey Smith, a source of encouragement, partnership, and love, who brought me to the place where the words flowed. This book would not exist as it is without you.

The women in the picture. The heart broken by our goodbyes led me to discover the boy, learn how to hold him, and be held by him in return.

Devon Smiddy, Mindy Jensen, Jamie Leite, Karla Angel, Carolyn Lohr, and Rebecca Joseph, early readers whose feedback inspired me and greatly enhanced the story.

Mastermind colleagues Megan Taylor Morrison, Will Drucker, Rachel Hegarty, Elizabeth Tuazon, and Hang Zhao, essential sources of encouragement, feedback, and support.

Kristin Robinson, my co-host on the Cultivating Courage podcast, where I spoke this book into existence so many times it finally became reality.

Coaches Bob Conlin, Rodney Mueller, and Karla Angel, standing for me to see outside the stories and live outside my comfort zone.

Leaders, teammates, and trainers at Accomplishment Coaching, Landmark, and C1, each a beacon of possibility and freedom.

Allie Daigle, who illustrated these ideas into such astonishing and powerful images, a collaboration that surpassed all expectation.

Enrica Barberis, who wrapped it together perfectly.

The many philosophers and writers whose words and insight have transformed my life.

So many friends and loved ones, for their encouragement and support through the years.

My future wife and children, a dream worth leaving all stories behind for.

The boy. You are loved beyond measure.

About the Author

Matthew Maxwell is dedicated to human freedom, joy, and connection and to our stewardship of the earth. Once a meat-loving Mormon lawyer, he is now a spiritually-curious writer, speaker, coach, and vegetarian. He founded and leads Hearthstone Coaching, helping individuals, teams, and organizations to clarify and create what matters most to them. Find out more at ThisIsHearthstone.com.

Matt is a graduate of the University of Hawaii and the University of Chicago Law School. In his free time, he enjoys meditating, walking in the woods, acting in plays, dancing like nobody's watching, and adventuring outside of his comfort zone.

Connect with Matt and discover more resources at HowtoHoldaCockroach.com.

About the Illustrator

Allie Daigle is an illustrator based in Connecticut who works in both traditional and new mediums. She earned a BFA from the University of Connecticut School of Fine Arts in 2017 and has since been building a career in freelance illustration. She works on a variety of projects, ranging from children's books to product ideation sketches to craft beer labels. Her artwork is defined by unique pen work, intriguing use of color, and quirky character design. Allie constantly seeks new challenges that push her artistic growth.

See more of her work here:
alliedaigle.com
instagram.com/a_bagel

Business inquiries only:
alliedaigleillustrations@gmail.com

Made in United States
North Haven, CT
14 January 2023

31073986R00067